remember

VALLEY FORGE

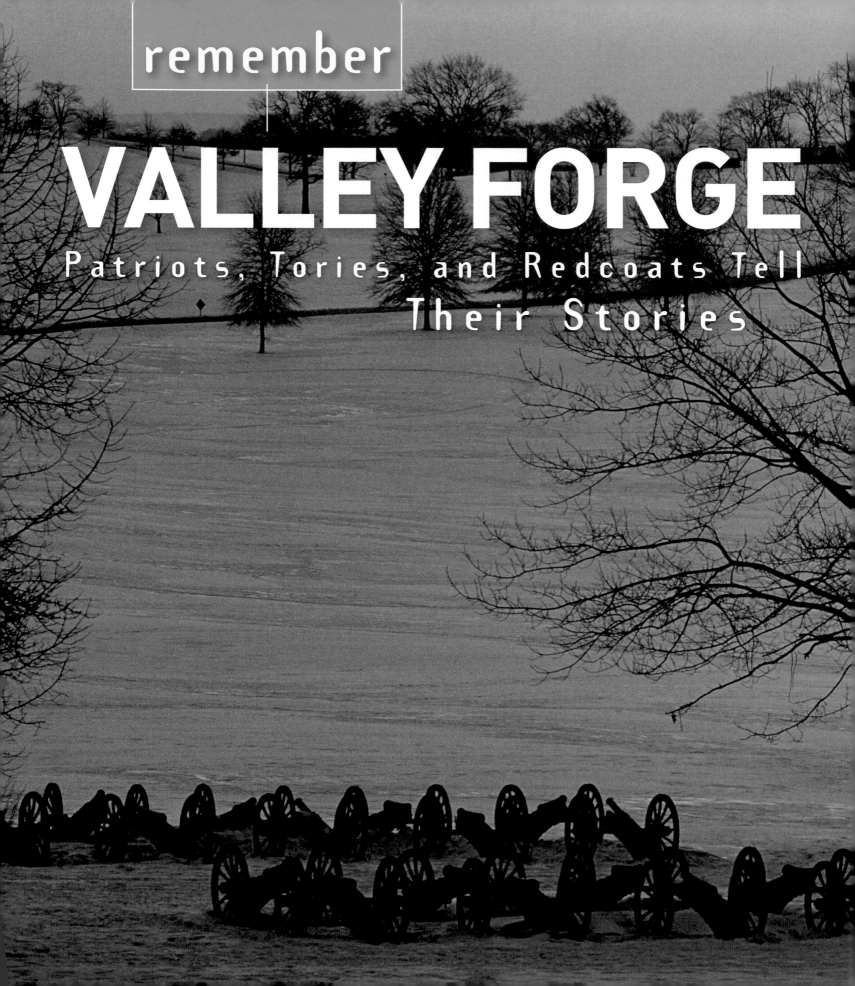

remember
VALLEY FORGE
Patriots, Tories, and Redcoats Tell Their Stories

Thomas B. Allen

with a foreword by **Thomas Fleming,**
Senior Scholar, The American Revolution Center®

NATIONAL GEOGRAPHIC

WASHINGTON, D.C.

To my grandchildren

STAFF FOR THIS BOOK
Suzanne Patrick Fonda, *Project Editor*
David M. Seager, *Art Director*
Callie Broaddus, *Associate Designer*
Lori Epstein, *Senior Photo Editor*
Justin Morrill, The M Factory, Inc., *Map Research and Production*
Paige Towler, *Editorial Assistant*
Jennifer A. Thornton, *Managing Editor*
R. Gary Colbert, *Production Director*
Lewis R. Bassford, *Production Manager*
Jennifer Hoff, *Manager, Production Services*

PUBLISHED BY THE NATIONAL GEOGRAPHIC SOCIETY
Gary E. Knell, *President and CEO*
John M. Fahey, *Chairman of the Board*
Melina Gerosa Bellows, *Chief Education Officer*
Declan Moore, *Chief Media Officer*
Hector Sierra, *Senior Vice President and General Manager, Book Division*

SENIOR MANAGEMENT TEAM, KIDS PUBLISHING AND MEDIA
Nancy Laties Feresten, *Senior Vice President;* Jennifer Emmett, *Vice
President, Editorial Director, Kids Books;* Julie Vosburgh Agnone, *Vice
President, Editorial Operations;* Rachel Buchholz, *Editor and Vice Presi-
dent,* NG Kids *magazine;* Michelle Sullivan, *Vice President, Kids Digital;*
Eva Absher-Schantz, *Design Director;* Jay Sumner, *Photo Director;* Hannah
August, *Marketing Director;* R. Gary Colbert, *Production Director*

DIGITAL
Anne McCormack, *Director;* Laura Goertzel, Sara Zeglin, *Producers;* Jed
Winer, *Special Projects Assistant;* Emma Rigney, *Creative Producer;* Brian
Ford, *Video Producer;* Bianca Bowman, *Assistant Producer;* Natalie Jones,
Senior Product Manager

Text is set in ITC New Baskerville.

The National Geographic Society is one of the world's largest nonprofit scientific and educational organizations. Founded in 1888 to "increase and diffuse
geographic knowledge," the Society's mission is to inspire people to care
about the planet. It reaches more than 400 million people worldwide each
month through its official journal, *National Geographic,* and other magazines;
National Geographic Channel; television documentaries; music; radio; films;
books; DVDs; maps; exhibitions; live events; school publishing programs;
interactive media; and merchandise. National Geographic has funded more
than 10,000 scientific research, conservation, and exploration projects and
supports an education program promoting geographic literacy.

For more information, please visit nationalgeographic.com,
call 1-800-NGS LINE (647-5463), or write to the following address:

NATIONAL GEOGRAPHIC SOCIETY
1145 17th Street N.W.
Washington, D.C. 20036-4688 U.S.A.

Visit us online at nationalgeographic.com/books

For librarians and teachers: ngchildrensbooks.org

More for kids from National Geographic: kids.nationalgeographic.com

For information about special discounts for bulk purchases, please contact
National Geographic Books Special Sales: ngspecsales@ngs.org

**National Geographic supports K–12 educators with ELA Common Core
Resources. Visit natgeoed.org/commoncore for more information.**

Printed in China
15/RRDS/1

ACKNOWLEDGMENTS
My thanks, first of all, to Thomas Fleming, who not only wrote the foreword
but also steered me away from errors. Another outstanding helper on this
book was Scott Houting, museum specialist at Valley Forge National Historical Park. And my thanks go to everyone on the Geographic staff (listed
at left), who did their usual superb work to produce this book.

The Library of Congress cataloged the 2007 edition as follows:
Allen, Thomas B.
  Remember Valley Forge: Patriots, Tories, and Redcoats tell their
  stories/Thomas B. Allen.
   p. cm. — (The remember series)
  ISBN 978-1-4263-0149-0 (trade) — ISBN 978-1-4263-0150-6 (library)
1. Washington, George, 1732–1799—Headquarters—Pennsylvania—Valley
Forge—Juvenile literature. 2. Valley Forge (Pa.)—History—
18th century—Juvenile literature. 3. United States. Continental Army—
History—Juvenile literature. 4. Pennsylvania—History—Revolution,
1775–1783—Juvenile literature. 5. United States—History—Revolution,
1775–1783—Juvenile literature. I. Title.
  E234.A44 2007
  973.3'341—dc22

                         2007024821

2015 paperback edition ISBN: 978-1-4263-2250-1
2015 reinforced library edition ISBN: 978-1-4263-2355-3

*COVER: In the cold and snow of Valley Forge, General George Washington
looks upon his soldiers and sees many of them without shoes or "blankets
to lie upon."*

*TITLE PAGE: At Valley Forge National Historical Park, cannon cluster
around a campfire. Fortifications surrounded the Continental Army's
winter quarters, awaiting a British attack that never came.*

From this stone house at Valley Forge, General Washington commanded the Continental Army. Besides issuing orders, he wrote frequent pleas to Congress, asking for aid for his starving men. Washington rented the house from an owner of the forge that gave the valley its name.

A few years ago, an old friend asked me to serve as an escort when he and his family came to Philadelphia to explore the history of America's birth as a nation. He told me how fondly he remembered his boyhood explorations of historic sites, such as Colonial Williamsburg and Gettysburg, with his grandfather, a professor of history. My friend was hoping to impart this fascination with America's past to his two sons and daughter.

We spent the morning touring Independence Hall and the Liberty Bell pavilion, while I talked about the doubts and hesitations that tormented the politicians before they finally declared America independent in 1776. That courageous decision did not mean the end of their worries. They now had to govern this new country, which sprawled from Boston to Savannah, and somehow win a war with Great Britain, the most powerful nation on the globe.

At lunch in City Tavern, I discussed the latest historical thinking on the American Army in the Revolution. Along with men of English descent, there were soldiers with Irish, German, African-American, and Native American backgrounds in their ranks. All played important roles in the exhausting eight-year struggle for independence.

In the afternoon, we drove to Valley Forge. On the way, I talked about the importance of the place we were going to visit. Here was where the Revolutionary struggle almost collapsed— and was miraculously reborn. I emphasized how vital the soldiers at Valley Forge were to

eventual victory. They were "regulars," most of whom had enlisted for the duration of the war. In 1776, General Washington had described them as "an army to look the enemy in the face." Without them, civilians would have lost heart and abandoned the struggle.

When we reached Valley Forge, we gazed across the rolling landscape while I asked the visitors to imagine thousands of men living in smokey wooden huts and marching on the parade ground. I pictured days when drifting snow made it hard to walk. I described the soldiers's lean, half-starved faces, their tattered uniforms, and their bare, often bleeding feet.

Then we drove to the small stone house where General Washington and his wife, Martha, and the general's aides spent the winter. It was here that Washington wrote tormented letters to Congress, urging them to feed and clothe the army. It was also here that he worked to defeat a conspiracy to force him to resign.

We looked across the fields and woods toward Philadelphia, 20 miles away. That was where the British Army spent the winter, warm and well fed. Knowing this made the Continental Army's ordeal at Valley Forge even more meaningful. "You can feel it, you can almost see what they went through," my friend said. "Here's where we can learn what it means to be an American."

Thomas B. Allen's book captures this mysterious power of Valley Forge as a symbol of America's spiritual strength. It is as good as a visit, and it will make an actual visit unforgettable.

Thomas Fleming
Senior Scholar
The American Revolution Center®

After the British capture of New York City, General Washington retreats across
New Jersey in the fall of 1776. Throughout the Revolution, New Jersey
was a battleground, not only between the British and the Continental Armies
but also between Patriots and pro-British Tories.

the road to valley forge

When he was a teenager, George Washington discovered an unexpected skill: He could read the landscape, looking at its ridges and hills, and then transfer what he saw to paper. Many years later, as General Washington in the American Revolution, he wrote about the lack of dependable battlefield maps. He solved that problem by making his own maps, based on "such sketches as I could trace from my own Observations."

In December 1776, looking at the landscape as a general, he placed the Delaware River between himself and the British Army by setting up his camp at a place in Pennsylvania called the Falls of Trenton, directly across the river from Trenton, New Jersey. The British had driven Washington's army away from New York. Now they were aiming at their next conquest, Philadelphia, where the Continental Congress met.

For a year, Philadelphia would be the prize—sought by the British and shielded by Washington's army. The fighting and maneuvering would go on until, finally, in December 1777 the British Army would settle into the city for a winter of feasting and fun while a ragged American Army would enter Valley Forge.

While Washington's men camped along the Delaware River during that dark December of 1776, Tom Paine, a journalist and pamphlet writer, looked at what he saw and wrote: "These are the times that try men's souls. The summer soldier and the sunshine patriot will, in this crisis, shrink from the service of their country; but he that stands by it now, deserves the love and thanks of man and woman." He had no way of knowing that the worst was yet to come.

Usually, the American Revolution is seen as a war between the British colonies in America and the British in England. In fact, it was a true civil war, with the people of the Colonies divided, neighbor fighting neighbor. Many Americans believed that George III, King of Great Britain, had been chosen by God to reign. They revered the king and saw the Revolution as an effort by

Tom Paine

Tory soldier

George Washington

dangerous rebel insurgents to wrest control from the rightful government. These people were known as Loyalists or Tories. Thousands of Tories formed military units under British command. The Rebels (or Patriots, as they called themselves) saw it another way. They had once been loyal subjects of the king. But now, in the words of the Declaration of Independence—proclaimed in Philadelphia only months before—they believed him a tyrant, "unfit to be the ruler of a free people."

Now, in December of 1776, things looked bad for General Washington's army and the cause of independence. Members of Congress, fearing that Washington would not be able to stop the British advance on their capital city, began to flee Philadelphia. And as winter set in and it began to look as if they might be fighting on the losing side, Washington's army was shrinking day by day.

"I think the game is pretty near up," Washington wrote his brother John on December 18. A British officer, Captain Francis Lord Rawdon, agreed, writing around the same time: "The fact is their army is broken all to pieces. . . . it is well nigh over with them."

To understand what kind of an army Washington had, let's go back to an April day in 1775, when 14-year-old Joseph Plumb Martin was plowing on his grandfather's Connecticut farm. Joseph heard town bells ringing and guns firing, summoning people to the village green to be told exciting news: In Lexington and Concord, two towns near Boston, British troops had clashed with Massachusetts militiamen. The Revolutionary War had begun!

Joseph wanted to enlist, but not until he was 15 did he get permission from his grandparents. He became a soldier in June 1776, enlisting for just six months in the Connecticut militia. He did not have a uniform, nor was he given much training. As a farm boy, he knew how to handle a gun, and his grandfather gave him a musket to carry off to war. He also gave him a Bible and a knapsack full of clothing and food.

Joseph Martin was like other men, young and old, in the Colonies. They signed up for limited enlistments in their own state militias and were led by local officers. Some of the militiamen wore buckskin made of deer they had

April 19, 1775: Massachusetts militiamen answer a volley from British Redcoats on the Lexington Green. Eight Americans are killed. The British, seeking Patriot weapons and ammunition, march on to Concord, where more militiamen stand and fight. The Revolutionary War has begun.

slain. Older men had on the faded uniforms left from when they had fought on the British side against the French 20 years before. Some wore homespun—clothes woven of flax or wool spun by wives and mothers on the home spinning wheel. Those clothes, Joseph knew, were symbols of protest. Many Americans had refused to buy cloth and other products from the king's England.

Each of these militias had its own organizational structure and its own rules. And because they were made up of patriotic citizens who were only part-time soldiers, enlistment times—like Joseph Martin's six months—were short. Washington's army had not been defeated by the British in New York during the autumn of 1776. The general had managed a wise military retreat, preserving his men to fight another day. Now, however, he knew further retreat would lead to the loss of the capital. He needed a victory, and he had a new enemy: the calendar. Enlistments for many of his troops would end on January 1, 1777.

Washington had set up spy networks and was fighting a secret war inside the battlefield war. Now his spies told him that the Redcoats (as the British soldiers were called after the red uniforms they wore) and their hired German allies, the Hessians, were scattered across New Jersey in small units, with Hessians stationed in and around Trenton. (Hessians were so called because they came from Hesse, then a principality in what is now Germany. The prince of Hesse had hired them out in a deal with King George.)

Hessian soldier

American soldiers haul a cannon-carrying boat ashore during Washington's crossing of the icy Delaware River. The army landed early on the morning of December 26, 1776, and marched through a sleet storm to launch a surprise attack on Hessians holding Trenton. In a fierce battle, Washington won a desperately needed victory.

Washington sent men 30 miles up the icy Delaware River and 30 miles down. The men were told to collect all the boats they could find. Boats not collected were to be destroyed so British soldiers and their Hessian and Loyalist allies couldn't use them. Washington particularly wanted Durham boats, named after the engineer credited with designing them. The flat-bottomed boats, 40 to 60 feet long, hauled freight to and from Philadelphia. Each boat, Washington figured, could hold as many as 40 armed men.

Washington also told his officers to alert their men to a suspicious cattle seller who was reported to be stealing cattle and selling the meat to the Hessians in Trenton. On December 22, that very cattle rustler, John Honeyman, wandered near American lines and was captured after a scuffle.

Washington told the captors to bring him Honeyman for questioning. In a private meeting, the rustler—in reality a member of Washington's spy network—told Washington how many Hessians were in Trenton and added that they were planning a Christmas party. Washington then arranged for Honeyman to escape so that he could go to one of his beef customers, the officer in command of the Hessians, and tell him not to worry about those tired, starving, and poorly armed Americans across the river. Modern spies call this "planting misinformation."

Each day, guards around the American camp were given a new password, used to make sure anyone coming into the camp was a friend, not a foe. On December 25, the Christmas Day password was "Victory or Death." At midnight, Washington and his men boarded the seized Durham boats and crossed the

Delaware. Washington knew that by morning his men would either be dead, captured, or celebrating a victory won by a desperate and daring attack.

Wind-whipped sleet buffeted the boats, freezing the Americans and keeping the Hessians inside their quarters. On the other side of the river, Washington's men still had a 9-mile march to Trenton. Staggering along the road, John Greenwood, a 16-year-old soldier, "was so be-numbed with cold that I wanted to go to sleep"—the first sign that a person is freezing to death. Luckily, he forced himself to stay awake and stumbled on.

The morning was still dark when the Americans struck, startling the sleeping Hessians. In a furious battle that lasted about 45 minutes, the Americans killed 21 Hessians, wounded 90, and took about 900 prisoners. Four Americans were wounded. The only American deaths were 2 men who had frozen on the night march to Trenton.

In Princeton, New Jersey, on January 3, 1777, Washington's exhausted troops—including many volunteers who fought even though their enlistments had expired—won another battle. Washington had achieved his goal. Philadelphia remained in Patriot hands.

From Princeton, Washington led his army—down to 2,500 men from the 14,000 or more when he first took command in 1775—to the heights of Morristown, New Jersey, where they would camp until spring. Armies then usually did not fight in cold weather. Instead, they went into winter quarters.

Colonel Johann Gottlieb Rall, the Hessian commander, lies mortally wounded at the feet of Washington's horse after the Trenton victory. The imagined scene shows a wounded American officer (below, right), possibly Lieutenant James Monroe, a future U.S. President.

Soldiers at Valley Forge could get 100 lashes for stealing, attempting to desert, striking an officer, and other offenses. A deserting drummer boy's sentence was cut to 50 lashes because of his youth.

Again, Washington had found exactly what he needed: The Morristown camp was only a two-day march to the British in New York City, but it lay behind the Watchung Mountains, which formed a natural defense against surprise attack.

Many men saw no point in spending a cold, idle winter in Morristown. They deserted, risking execution by hanging if they were found, brought back, and convicted. Washington, determined to make the army better disciplined, had received from Congress approval of new and harsher corporal (bodily) punishment for violating rules of behavior (called Articles of War). The new rules, which Washington had specifically asked for, increased punishment for various offenses from a maximum number of 39 lashes to a maximum of 100.

Soldiers whose enlistments had ended headed back to their farms and towns. Washington, watching his men walk off, knew he had to build a new army. He also had to keep the British from discovering how small his army had become. To, as he put it, "make small numbers appear large," he frequently sent out units that appeared here and there around Morristown. The British did not realize that many of these patrols were made up of the same men marching out of camp again and again. The trick worked. British spies reported that Washington had more than 5,000 able-bodied men, when in fact, thousands were unfit to fight or even forage.

Members of Congress, meanwhile, returned to Philadelphia and took up the task of building a new Continental Army. Congress, which did not have authority to levy taxes, asked the states to enlist men and pay for their weapons, clothing, and other equipment. Some states required their soldiers to provide their own muskets. Congress asked the states to sign men up for three years. By June, Washington's army numbered 10,000 soldiers.

One of the new soldiers was Private Joseph Plumb Martin, who had ended his enlistment in the Connecticut militia after fighting in battles in New York. In the spring, after a dull winter at home, he enlisted in the Continental Army as a private, the lowest rank, and headed with his regiment to join Washington's forces. He liked being a soldier, he later wrote, even though the "whole time is

George Washington directs his troops at Brandywine Creek, near Philadelphia. Outmaneuvered by the British, Washington lost the battle. He retreated, keeping his army unbroken. The battle cleared the way for the British to take Philadelphia.

spent in marches (especially night marches), watching, starving, and, in cold weather, freezing and sickness."

On May 28, 1777, Washington led his men out of winter quarters and began maneuvering around New Jersey in moves aimed at protecting Philadelphia while avoiding a major battle. General William Howe, commander of the British troops in America, was also in New Jersey.

Howe had a low opinion of the rebellious colonists. When "they find they are not supported in their frantic ideas by the more moderate," he wrote, they would end the Revolution "from fear of punishment." He decided to outwit Washington by not marching to Philadelphia. Instead, he took his army back to New York City. There, his brother, Admiral Richard Howe, was assembling a fleet of more than 250 ships that would take General Howe and 15,000 men south to Chesapeake Bay. They would land at the head of the Elk River in Maryland, and march on to Philadelphia, about 50 miles to the northeast. By the time the Howe brothers' fleet reached land, Washington had moved his troops closer to Philadelphia to block the British path to the city.

But, on September 11, 1777, Washington was outmaneuvered and defeated at Brandywine Creek, southwest of Philadelphia, opening the way for General Howe and most of his troops to enter the city. Members of the Continental Congress fled again, first to Lancaster, and then to York, Pennsylvania. Washington tried a surprise attack on Howe's troops in Germantown, outside Philadelphia. Many on both sides were killed in the ferocious attack. But once again Washington's men had to retreat.

William Howe

General Washington and Major General the Marquis de Lafayette inspect
troops at Valley Forge. When the French officer volunteered at age 19 to serve
in the Continental Army, Congress had no money to pay his way to America.
So Lafayette bought his own ship. He was wounded at Brandywine.

winter quarters

General Washington was reading the frozen landscape at Whitemarsh, near Philadelphia, and thinking about the best place for his army's winter quarters when members of Congress, looking for another victory, began telling him that he and his army should spend the winter fighting Redcoats and driving them from Philadelphia. "We shall be able during the Winter to strike a bold Stroke against Mr. Howe," predicted William Duer, a delegate to Congress from New York. When he wrote to Washington, Duer was living in the safe haven of York, Pennsylvania, far from Howe and his army.

William Duer

Congress sent a committee to talk to Washington about "the best and most practicable means for carrying on a winter's campaign." What Congress was not doing was figuring a way to get food, shoes, tents, and clothing to the starving men of the Continental Army.

Washington's army of 9,000 or so soldiers had spent the fall holding off attack. The British were in control of New York and Philadelphia, as well as the waterways that connected the two cities. And the army "was now not only starved but naked, the greatest part were not only shirtless and barefoot, but destitute of all other clothing, especially blankets," Private Joseph Plumb Martin later wrote.

Dragoons, as soldiers on horseback were called, did not have enough horses. When some dragoon officers and enlisted men stole horses from suspected Tories, Washington was outraged, warning that horse thieves would be executed. But Washington was even angrier at Congress for suggesting that he should lead his starving, shoeless men to fight the British in the cold of winter.

Joseph Plumb Martin

The soldiers were victims of a breakdown of the supply system that Congress, with its limited authority, had set up. Army officers, along with civilians who were outside military control, bought supplies, such as barrels of flour and barrels of salted fish, and kept them in storehouses miles behind the

Valley Forge soldiers warm themselves around campfires. Washington's officers called the winter quarters "a Place that abounds with nothing but poverty and Wretchedness." Of 756 men in one brigade, 450 were declared "unfit for Duty for want of shoes and other clothing."

Much of the time men lived on flour-and-water "fire cakes," making plates, knives, and forks, such as these, of little use. Some cuts of meat were made edible only by boiling them a long time.

army's camps. The suppliers were supposed to hire wagons and horses to deliver the supplies from the storehouses to the camps. But delivery men and suppliers were cheating, stealing supplies and selling them to civilians. This meant that supplies would mysteriously disappear somewhere between the storehouses and the army camps.

As new men like Private Martin entered the army and increased its size, the supplies did not increase. Congress had tinkered with the system, but the shortages continued. The army general in charge of supplies resigned, and another supply official quit after telling Washington that the army storehouse had only 90 pairs of shoes available.

Meat was the most important food in the soldiers' diet. In October 1777, the army suppliers had about 3,000 head of cattle in Pennsylvania. Washington knew that was not enough to keep his men fed even for a month, because each week it was necessary to butcher at least 800 cattle to feed them. Another important food was bread, and bakers needed 400 barrels of flour a week to make enough bread. But there was a shortage of flour because farmers were demanding higher and higher prices for their wheat. And even if army suppliers could buy the wheat, they could not find the wagons to haul it. Farmers in New Jersey and Pennsylvania were hiding their wagons to keep them from being taken away. Toward the end of November 1777, one supply officer wrote to another: "Not a single barrel of flour. . .have I to deliver out to the troops this morning. . .exert yourself. . . or all's over."

Fearful members of state assemblies in Pennsylvania and New Jersey also called on Washington, urging him to invade Philadelphia immediately and drive out the British. "I can assure those Gentlemen," Washington later wrote, "that it is much easier" to talk about a winter war while sitting "in a comfortable room by a good fire side than to occupy a cold bleak hill and sleep under frost and Snow without Cloaths or Blankets."

Washington was dealing with a Congress in York that was far different from the Congress that had passed the Declaration of Independence. Many of the York members had not even met Washington. Only six of the congressmen in York had been among the members who in 1775 had voted for Washington to be commander in chief.

This receipt is for goods shipped to Valley Forge from Fairfield, Connecticut. Connecticut is called the "Provision State" because it supplied so much to the Revolution.

While in York, Congress passed the Articles of Confederation, which supposedly turned the separate colonies into the United States of America. But it would take nearly four years for the Articles to be ratified (approved) by all the states. Meanwhile, Congress had little power over the states—or, it turned out, over General Washington. He believed that he and his generals, not Congress, should decide military matters, and he had made up his mind: winter quarters, not winter war.

On the night of December 11, men left their camp in the hills of Whitemarsh and began pushing loaded wagons into the cold waters of the Schuylkill River.

Albigence Waldo

They placed boards between the wagons. Through the night, the army crossed the river on this wagon bridge. Washington led his men down a steep road to a hamlet called Gulph Mills, where the army camped for several days.

Albigence Waldo, an army doctor from Connecticut, looked around at the Gulph Mills camp and wrote in his diary: "There comes a Soldier, his bare feet are seen thro' his worn out Shoes, his legs nearly naked from the tatter'd remains of an only pair of stockings, his Breeches [pants] not sufficient to cover his nakedness, his Shirt hanging in Strings, his hair dishevell'd. . . exhausted by fatigue, hunger and Cold. . . ." In the face of that soldier, Waldo saw the faces of all the men, whipped by a "cold & piercing" wind, who followed General Washington down a steep, frozen road to a place called Valley Forge.

Washington had found a winter quarters site that would both keep his army safe and worry the British. Despite its name, Valley Forge, 20 miles northwest of Philadelphia, was high ground, not a valley. The site was near the main road between York and Philadelphia, giving Congressmen the protection they wanted. With Washington's army so close, British soldiers knew they could be attacked when they went out from the city, foraging the farms around Philadelphia.

Valley Forge was the name of a village that had been built around one of the many ironworks in that area. Besides forges, the ironworks had had a "slitting mill" for paring, or slicing, bars of iron into rods from which nails were made. The rushing waters of Valley Creek had powered the slitting mill, a sawmill, and a gristmill, where farmers had their grain ground into flour. But when Washington and his army set up quarters there, the ironworks were in ruin. They had been burned to the ground by the British to keep them from being used to make war supplies. Valley Creek, flowing north into the Schuylkill River, curves between two steep, forested hills called Mount Joy and Mount Misery, which, along with the river, formed natural defense barriers. On a broad ridge east of Mount Joy, Washington envisioned his main encampment.

One of his generals called the forests a wilderness. To Washington, the forests were providers of building materials, and to Colonel Louis LeBeque Duportail, the ridge was a huge fortress. Duportail, a French military engineer (who also spied for France), was one of many Europeans who volunteered to aid the Americans. Others included two Germans—Friedrich von Steuben and Johann de Kalb—and two officers from Poland—Casimir Pulaski and Thaddeus Kosciuzko. The foreign officer closest to Washington was the 20-year-old Marquis de Lafayette of France.

Duportail designed an outer line of defenses by placing redoubts—small forts for 50 or so men—on a highland ridge that overlooked likely routes for British attack. The redoubts could be manned quickly because they were near the site where most of the soldiers would be living. This outer defense line could probably hold against any attack. But if that line were overrun, there was an inner line. The Americans would be able to pull back, jump into wide trenches, and, protected behind mounds of dirt, fire down on advancing foes. Cannon could be brought up to add to the firepower.

Washington had divided his army into 12-man squads. Now, in a special

Soldiers build their log huts, following Washington's plan. They cut down thousands of trees, transforming a forest into barren hillsides. Building began in December. On February 8, Washington reported that "most of the men are in tolerable good Hutts."

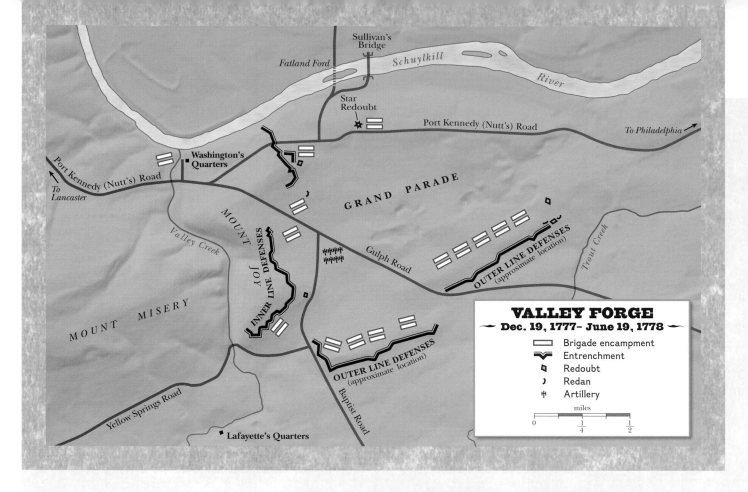

At Valley Forge Washington found a site that would keep his army well defended against attack. The winter quarters encompassed a triangle of about 2,000 acres. Surrounding the encampment were an Outer Line and an Inner Line, which bristled with cannon and trenches. Men drilled on the Grand Parade.

order, he told each squad exactly how to build its hut. Each hut was to be 16 feet long and 14 feet wide, with side walls 6 ½ feet high. At the rear of each hut there was to be a fireplace, made of wood and lined with clay. At the front there was to be a door "made of split oak slabs, unless boards can be procured." Spaces between the logs were to be filled with mud, clay, or moss. Roofs varied: slabs of logs, turf, evergreen boughs, straw, pieces of tents. Some huts had small windows made of oiled paper.

Washington planned for a "city" of nearly 2,000 huts, arranged in streets, with officers' huts forming a line behind the troops' huts. The troops would build huts for the officers, who would share huts; the lower the rank, the greater the number of sharers. Generals and their aides moved into nearby farmhouses, becoming surprise guests of the owners. The forest began to disappear as men hacked away, selecting logs for their huts and finding smaller timber for campfires. Some carried the hut logs on their backs. Others made sleds, strapped themselves to them, and pulled loads of logs through snow or mud to the hut sites.

Tom Paine, the pamphlet writer, came to Valley Forge and watched the soldiers working "like a family of beavers, every one busy; some carrying logs, others mud, and the rest plastering them together." Many soldiers did not follow the general's orders completely, and so, as Paine said, Washington's orderly hut city was actually "a curious collection of buildings," numbering about a thousand.

The builders of those huts were from every state. Some were boys as young as 12, and some were men in their 50s and 60s. Most soldiers were white, but among them were Indians and African Americans. Washington, a slave-owner, had taken a slave name Billy with him to war. At first, Washington resisted the enlistment of black soldiers, even though many had fought at Bunker Hill in the battle for Boston in 1775. But, after the British offered freedom to slaves who joined the Loyalists, Washington changed his mind, allowing blacks to become American soldiers. At Valley Forge, he approved a Rhode Island proposal to raise a regiment of freed slaves for the Continental Army.

While the huts were being built, Washington lived in his marquee—a large tent that included a sleeping area, an office, and a dining area. Atop it flew his blue commander-in-chief flag with its 13 stars. He stayed in the tent until just before Christmas, when he moved into the stone house that belonged to an owner of the ruined forge. The house became the headquarters for the entire Continental Army.

The soldiers managed to cut down thousands of trees and build their huts, though their stomachs were empty and rags were wrapped around many a bleeding foot. Shoeless Private Martin had made moccasins from "a small piece of raw cowhide" on the march to Valley Forge. But the "hard edges so galled my ankles. . .that it was with much difficulty and pain that I could wear

More than 500 "free negroes" were among the soldiers at Valley Forge.

them. [T]he only alternative. . .was. . .to go barefoot, as hundreds of my companions had to, till they might be tracked by their blood upon the rough frozen ground." He and his comrades were "weak, starved, and naked. . .in the midst of a plentiful country."

He was right. There was plenty of food nearby, produced by the farms that fed Philadelphia. But two large armies were competing for that food. The Americans paid with paper money, called "Continentals," issued by the Continental Congress. People did not trust the pieces of paper, inspiring a new saying: "not worth a Continental." The British paid with gold or silver. So most of the area's wagons, horses, forage, and food went to Howe's army.

The Pennsylvania General Assembly, stepping into the crisis, gave Washington the power to buy whatever he needed. If a farmer refused to sell because he did not trust Continental currency, the farmer's grain or livestock

Finding suitable trees for buildidng huts was not a problem, but there was a shortage of tools and nails. Branches, too small for use in construction, became fuel for campfires and for fireplaces inside the huts. Here, a wagon filled with logs rolls past a sentry.

Buying food for Valley Forge soldiers was difficult because farmers distrusted paper money issued by the Continental Congress. Like other states, Pennsylvania printed its own bills, which carried promises that the paper could be exchanged for British or Spanish coins, known as "hard money."

would be taken and the farmer would be a given a piece of paper promising the proper price at a given date in the future. But even with this power, Washington had to watch his men starve, for the once-ample food in the area was rapidly disappearing. Washington found that he did not even have enough food on hand to provide rations for men to carry in their knapsacks when they left camp to forage or to attack British foragers. At least one soldier was killed by a farmer who caught him stealing. A supply officer, convicted of robbing from Valley Forge's scanty food stores, was tied backward on a horse and, to a roll of drums, sent out of camp, never to return.

On December 22, Washington wrote to Congress, saying that, because he did not have enough food, he could not defend Valley Forge. If "the Enemy crossed Schuylkill this Morning, as I had reason to expect from the intelligence I received at Four O'Clock last night, the Divisions which I ordered to be in readiness to march and meet them, could not have moved."

Next day, he wrote a more urgent letter: "I am now convinced, beyond a doubt that unless some great and capital change suddenly takes place. . . this Army must inevitably be reduced to one or other of these three things. Starve, dissolve, or disperse, in order to obtain subsistence in the best manner they can. . . ."

As he was sending his warning, he got new "information" from his spies: a large British force was heading out to forage. Despite the lack of food, he ordered his men to get ready to march out of Valley Forge and intercept the British. But he was told that the starving men had begun "a dangerous Mutiny," which alert officers had managed to put down. He wrote another letter to Congress, advising them that 2,898 men were "unfit for duty because they are bare foot and otherwise naked."

Congress was failing him. His starving men were turning mutinous. The enemy was close and threatening. But he had a secret weapon: the "information" he was getting from spies in Philadelphia.

Washington welcomes a congressional committee to Valley Forge. The congressmen saw for themselves the hardships that Washington had been reporting. The visit helped to improve both the army's supply system and Congress's trust of Washington.

spies, tories, and plotters

Major Benjamin Tallmadge, spymaster for Washington's agents in Philadelphia, took to the saddle at Valley Forge. As he later wrote, "I had to scour the country from the Schuylkill to the Delaware River, about five or six miles, for the double purpose of watching the movements of the enemy and preventing the disaffected from carrying supplies or provisions to Philadelphia."

The disaffected were Americans who, out of loyalty to the king or greed, chose to help the British. Among them were double agents, Americans who pretended to be working for Tallmadge while serving as spies for the British. And there was still another kind of double agent—one who spied for Tallmadge while seeming to be a spy for the British.

Benjamin Tallmadge

Tallmadge's spy ring was not the only espionage operation in the city. General Howe had his own spies and his own spymaster: Joseph Galloway, once a friend of Ben Franklin and a delegate to the First Continental Congress.

Galloway had become a Loyalist because he believed that to "be a subject of Great Britain is to be the finest subject of any civil community anywhere to be found on earth." As for rebels, they "rush into the blackest rebellion, and all the horrors of an unnatural civil war" for "the ill-shapen, diminutive brat, INDEPENDENCY."

While he was a congressman, Galloway had introduced a "Plan of Union," which would have loosened—but not severed—ties between Britain and the Colonies. His plan would have had the king appoint a president-general to run the Colonies, which would still have had their own legislature, under the control of Britain's Parliament. Like many Loyalists, Galloway believed that liberty for the Colonies did not mean independence from Britain. When Congress discarded the plan, Galloway wrote to a friend, "I stand here almost alone."

As Philadelphia's leading Loyalist, Galloway no longer stood alone. Besides being Howe's spymaster, Galloway was also the city's chief of police and the

Joseph Galloway

superintendent of the port, controlling imports and exports. Galloway thought that Americans would stay loyal to the king if they had an efficient government. He ran Philadelphia with great efficiency, hoping that after the British had put down the rebellion, the city would become a model for what the British called "the good Americans."

In his more secret role as a spymaster, Galloway preferred using deserters from Washington's army rather than citizens of Philadelphia. On some days, British reports on deserters said, "the rebels came in by 4s and 5s," and on other days there were as many as 50 or 60. The deserters, seeking food and comfort in Philadelphia, gave Galloway information about American foraging missions so that he could attack the foragers and keep food from the Valley Forge soldiers. At least two deserters—both Pennsylvanians with knowledge of the area—were caught by American patrols before they had a chance to become spies. They were hanged at Valley Forge after being tried by Continental Army officers.

General Howe was not Washington's only enemy. Some congressmen and some of his own generals had been muttering about Washington's failure to capture and hold New York and Philadelphia. Washington's triumphs at Trenton and Princeton were all but forgotten, especially after the American victory at Saratoga, New York, in October 1777—a victory that would convince France to become America's ally. Credit for winning that battle had gone to General Horatio Gates, although Major General Benedict Arnold, wounded in the fighting, deserved recognition for his daring attacks.

Washington's critics began talking secretly about replacing him with Gates. John Adams, who had nominated Washington as commander in chief in 1775, was among the congressmen who had lost faith in him. Rejoicing over the Saratoga victory, Adams, in a letter to his wife, Abigail, said he was glad that "a certain Citizen" [Washington, unnamed] had not been the winner at Saratoga. "Congress will appoint a Thanksgiving," Adams wrote, adding, "and one Cause of it ought to be that the Glory. . .is not immediately due to the Commander in Chief. . . ." Now, he sarcastically wrote, "We can allow a certain

John Adams

Major General Benedict Arnold, on his white horse, leads a charge at Freeman's Farm, one of the battles of Saratoga, a vital American victory. At the right, British Brigadier General Simon Fraser, mortally wounded, is carried off the battlefield. Legend has him shot by sharpshooter Tim Murphy, shown in the tree at left.

Citizen to be wise, virtuous, and good, without thinking him a Deity or a saviour."

One day in January 1778, Washington turned to Congressman Francis Dana of Massachusetts, who was visiting Valley Forge, and said, "Congress does not trust me. I cannot continue thus." Dana told him that most congressmen did support him. But by then, Congress had put Gates in charge of the Board of War, a congressional tool for running the army. At the same time, some officers formed what was called a "cabal," or secret plot, against Washington. But the majority of congressmen supported the commander in chief, and one of Washington's generals, John Cadwalader of Pennsylvania, even fought a duel with the leader of the cabal, Brigadier General Thomas Conway, shooting him in the face. Conway, thinking he was about to die, wrote a letter apologizing to Washington and calling him a "great and good man."

Washington eventually won back the trust of Congress, aided greatly by the efforts of his 22-year-old aide, John Laurens, son of Henry Laurens, president of Congress. John wrote to his father about the plot, giving him behind-the-scenes information and bringing him around to Washington's side.

Washington's greatest worry was that he would lose the trust of his hungry men. Doctor Albigence Waldo had gone around the camp, trying to get an idea of the soldiers' mood. A cry—"No meat! No Meat!"—would begin in one set of huts and echo throughout the camp. Waldo heard hooting and cackling as men from one end of the camp to the other began imitating owls and crows. This "confused Musick" seemed strangely threatening to Waldo. But he kept on walking around, asking, "What have you for your dinner, boys?"

"Nothing but Fire Cake and Water, Sir," they told him, referring to the blobs of water-soaked flour that they cooked over their campfires.

On February 19, Washington wrote to Virginia Governor Patrick Henry, whose stirring words, "Give me liberty or give me death!" had helped to launch the Revolution. "We. . .have had much cause to dread a general mutiny," Washington wrote. The mutiny did not happen, probably because, instead of mutinying, hundreds of men simply deserted. One shoeless private told his buddies he would desert as soon as he got shoes to walk away in. Washington

A Tory spy known as "Mr. Parker" slipped into Valley Forge and made this map. It shows "Washingtons Qtrs" (headquarters) along with key military sites, such as "2 guns & magazine" (storage place for ammunition) and small forts called "redoubts." The spy noted that the "Breastwork" (a fortification made of trees and dirt) was "4 feet high" and a defensive ditch was "2 feet wide 3 deep." Triangles mark inns and taverns.

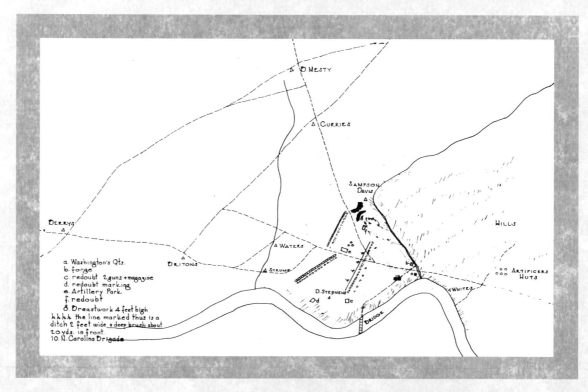

Saber drawn, an American dragoon rides by, followed by a bugler. The dragoon, or cavalryman, wears a helmet with a bearskin crescent. "Dragoon" comes from a fanciful name for the dragon-shaped hammer of a pistol, a typical weapon for dragoons. Horses starved along with the men of Valley Forge. About 1,500 horses died there.

repeatedly demanded counts of deserters from his officers. But, not wishing to be held responsible for desertions, they ignored the order. So the total number of deserters from Valley Forge is not known. Washington said he was "astonished, considering the sufferings the men have undergone, that more of them have not left us."

To try to ease that suffering by finding food, Washington told his officers to send out men who were in a condition to fight and forage and tell them to take whatever they could find, ignoring previous orders against seizing civilian property. Washington, infuriated at Americans who were selling to the British, ordered Major General Nathanael Greene to make "severe examples of a few to deter others." Civilians attempting to drive cattle and sheep to Philadelphia were captured and given 200 or 250 lashes. Their animals were taken to Valley Forge.

Washington, who once had threatened to execute horse thieves, now ordered Greene to "take, Carry off and secure all such Horses as are suitable for Cavalry or for Draft and all Cattle and Sheep fit for Slaughter together with every kind of Forage." Instead of money, owners were given pieces of paper telling the owners how and where they could seek payment later. Greene, in one of his orders, told his men exactly what Washington wanted them to do: "You must forage the Country naked."

Still, the "market people," as the smugglers were called, "come and go as they please," said the commander of the Pennsylvania militia, which was outside Washington's direct control. The commander admitted that his own militiamen were thieves, "constantly stealing from the inhabitants and from one another."

Tories openly helped British troops who were foraging. One Pennsylvania village even declared that its residents were all supporters of the king. Many Tories took up arms against their fellow Americans. A 40-man Tory dragoon force left Philadelphia one day, raided villages about 25 miles away, killed several Pennsylvania militiamen, and returned to Philadelphia with wagons full of stolen goods.

Washington's foragers journeyed farther and farther from Valley Forge. One small force went to Bucks County, about 25 miles to the northeast. A dragoon unit rode to Delaware. Brigadier General Anthony Wayne led the largest unit, about 550 men, to southern New Jersey, where there was plenty of food and forage for animals but few available horses and wagons to carry forage back to Valley Forge. Nor could Wayne move anything on the Delaware and Schuylkill Rivers, which the British controlled for their New York-to-Philadelphia supply ships. Wayne realized that he had to round up cattle in New Jersey and deliver meat to Valley Forge on the hoof.

The British, alerted to Wayne's cattle drive, sent a mixed force of Tories and Redcoats to stop him—and get the livestock for themselves. They succeeded in rustling many of Wayne's cattle. Only about 50 cows made it to Valley Forge.

Though none of these efforts was perfect, near the end of February, Washington said he no longer feared that his army would be "experiencing a

famine." An officer reported that the camp had "a good supply" of food, and he hoped the food would last until at least mid-March.

In Philadelphia, meanwhile, there was no shortage of food or frolic. The British takeover of Philadelphia pleased most inhabitants. A majority of Quakers, distrusted by Patriots because of their anti-war views, felt more comfortable under British rule but did not necessarily become active Tories. Many merchants who had not been enthusiastic about the Revolution believed that the British would bring stability to the city. The city's upper class welcomed the British occupation. Countless Philadelphians invited British officers to parties and dances. For their part, officers, acting as Howe's Strolling Players, made the Southwark Theater their own playhouse. There they produced plays by Shakespeare and Molière.

Eighteen-year-old Rebecca Franks lived "the life of continued amusement," she said in a letter to a friend. Another pretty, flirtatious teenager, Peggy Shippen, was overjoyed when a handsome British officer, Captain John André, wrote poetry just for her.

General Howe enjoyed life in Philadelphia, preferring comfort to combat. His officers followed his ways, spending their time at a racetrack, at gambling tables, and at parties. They seemed to have forgotten that they were soldiers in the midst of a war.

Peggy Shippen

Drillmaster von Steuben sternly teaches Continental Army soldiers at
Valley Forge. All they knew about a bayonet, he said, was how to
use it as a skewer for grilling pieces of meat. A Prussian officer,
he volunteered to aid the Americans. Congress made him a major general.

CHAPTER 4

the making of an army

As winter dragged on, many officers at Valley Forge left the army, not by deserting, as enlisted men did, but by taking advantage of an officer's right to resign. Congress had set up rules like those of the British Army: Officers could legally quit anytime they wished. Most officers remained because of patriotism and a sense of personal honor. As one lieutenant wrote to his wife, "it Shall never be Said to my Children your father was a Coward." Those who resigned might be called cowards, but they saw themselves as men who were merely quitting a job. The idea of being a professional soldier did not appeal to many men in the Continental Army.

Washington was greatly troubled by the resignations. "No day, nor scarce an hour passes without the offer of a resignd Commission," Washington wrote. A few days later, Doctor Waldo noted in his diary that on a single day "upwards of fifty Officers. . .resigned their Commissions. All this is occation'd by Officers Families being so much neglected at home." The disheartened officers had another reason to leave: They had lost faith in the Continental Army.

At this low point, Washington welcomed the words of Tom Paine, who believed that the *continent* in Continental Army meant a *United* States, not a string of independent states. At the end of 1776, Paine had written his famous words about the times that try men's souls. One sentence especially caught the spirit that Washington hoped would stir his men in 1778: "Once more, we are. . .collecting; our new army at both ends of the continent is recruiting fast."

Our new army. Washington was rebuilding his army yet again. This time he was doing it with the help of Tom Paine's words and the military skills of Friedrich Wilhelm von Steuben.

Von Steuben had been in the royal army of Prussia (now part of Germany and Poland). After leaving the army, he traveled to Paris. There, in the summer

Friedrich Wilhelm von Steuben

A British soldier's main weapon was the Brown Bess (above, top), officially the "land service pattern musket." At a distance of 30 yards, it could fire a musket ball 5 inches into an oak tree. Many American soldiers carried muskets that were copies of the Brown Bess. With his musket, a soldier usually carried a box or leather case (above, center) for cartridges, which consisted of a ball and gunpowder wrapped in paper (above, lower). The steps in loading and firing a musket are shown in the art on the opposite page.

of 1777, he met Benjamin Franklin, who was trying to convince France to help the United States. Franklin, impressed by von Steuben, sent him to America with a letter introducing him to Washington. Von Steuben was a former captain when he met Franklin. In the letter, Franklin grandly described von Steuben as "a Lieutenant General in the King of Prussia's service."

With von Steuben came three French officers, including an interpreter and an engineer, Pierre L'Enfant. (When in 1790 Congress decided to build the nation's capital on the Potomac River, President Washington chose L'Enfant to design the city.) Von Steuben and the French officers, like the many other European officers who came to America, had left behind the kings they once had served, choosing to aid a revolution against a king.

An officer who was about to meet von Steuben at Valley Forge wondered what the Prussian could do to aid an army so badly equipped: "Our arms are in horrible condition, covered with rust, half of them without bayonets, many from which not a single shot can be fired." But von Steuben was more interested in the men than in their weapons. He could see that the soldiers of the Continental Army did not know how to work together. He wanted to teach each man how to be a soldier who could march in formation and fire a musket on command. He began with *Attention!* Von Steuben could speak only a little English, so his translator had to shout the command and tell the soldiers exactly what *"Attention!"* meant: "At this word, the soldier must be silent, stand firm and steady, moving neither hand nor foot. . . ."

The soldiers needed to learn how to move and fight in organized units. The basic unit was a platoon of 20 men. Two platoons made up a company, and 8 companies formed a battalion. At full strength, a regiment would have 2 battalions. This was more than a plan on paper. It was a plan for a battlefield and for survival. Soldiers in a tight, disciplined army had a better chance to live and win than soldiers who were loosely organized.

Such a strict organization was new to the Continental Army, whose military units varied in size and formation from state to state and even from unit to unit within a state. A "company" in some states might be larger than a "battalion,"

while in other states the reverse was the case. The Continental Army was still hardly more than a group of state militias.

Von Steuben started out with a "model company"—100 men, drawn from many regiments, who drilled on a large piece of cleared land called the Grand Parade. While he put the model company through its drills, soldiers and officers from all over the camp watched. He drilled his model company every day, no matter the weather. He also drastically changed the men's marching behavior. They usually had gone into battle in long lines (called "Indian file") and then formed ranks to fight. He showed them that, by marching in close-order (tight) ranks instead of straggling lines, they arrived ready to fight in units.

Speaking in a resounding, heavily accented voice— *"Von,* Two, *Tree,* Four. . . *Von,* Two, *Tree,* Four"—he sang out the cadence of the marching step. The step, Lieutenant George Ewing wrote in his journal, "is about half way betwixt Slow and Quick time, an easy and natural step." Ewing also liked the new drill for firing muskets all at the same time in response to a series of shouted commands that began with "Poise Firelock!" and ended with "Fire!"

Soon the Grand Parade was full of marching men, shouting drillmasters, and drummers practicing the beats they had learned from von Steuben.

Firing a musket takes about 15 seconds: The soldier bites open a cartridge, pours a little gunpowder into the musket's priming pan, pours the rest down the barrel, drops the ball after it (along with paper, which holds the ball in place). Then, with his ramrod, he shoves down the ball, powder, and paper. When he pulls the trigger, a flint scrapes metal, creating a spark that ignites powder in the pan. This explodes the barrel's gunpowder, propelling the ball toward its target.

General Washington and Major General von Steuben look over the soldiers trained by von Steuben. He noted that Americans, unlike European soldiers, had to be told "why you ought to do that" when he gave an order. He wrote a book on drills and discipline that remained a U.S. Army manual for more than 30 years.

Some of the drum signals, for instance, involved a "flam," a two-note drumbeat with accent on the second. The drum signal for "turn or face to the right" was one beat, followed by a flam; "to the left" was two beats and a flam.

Men from the model company reported to various regiments and taught their comrades. "I was kept constantly, when off other duty, engaged in learning the Baron de [von] Steuben's new Prussian exercise," Private Martin remembered. "[I]t was a continual drill."

Spring and new hope was coming to Valley Forge. In March, Washington appointed Major General Nathanael Greene as Quartermaster General (chief supply officer). Greene expanded the reach of the Quartermaster. Instead of buying horses from nearby sources, for example, he sent buyers to Virginia, where there were more horses—and lower prices. He personally promised several sellers that they would be paid; after the war, he fulfilled his promises with his own money.

Greene ordered the building of bridges and improvement of roads so that supplies could be moved faster. He also set up supply sites at storage depots near enough to serve the army on the march. At these depots were thousands of bushels of wheat, oats, corn, and rye. Soon Washington was able to report that "the army has been pretty well supplied." By April, von Steuben had so transformed the army that Congress, on Washington's recommendation, made von Steuben inspector general, with the rank of major general.

As warm breezes wafted through the camps, they carried the stink of garbage and the carcasses of countless horses that had starved to death during the winter. The huts of the unwashed men added to the smells. Disobeying Washington's specific orders—and risking the punishment of five lashes across the back—many men had relieved themselves in their huts instead of walking to latrines on freezing nights. Now came a new Washington order: Put windows in all huts and remove the mud in the chinks between logs so that the breezes can blow in and air the huts.

Washington often walked or rode around the camp and talked to the troops. One day he surprised a group of officers by joining them in playing the British game of cricket. Elsewhere, some of the men were playing "base," a bat-and-ball game that was a forerunner of American baseball. "Exercised in the afternoon," Lieutenant George Ewing wrote in his journal, and "in the intervals played at base."

Officers staged plays in a stone residence that served as the bake house. One play, *Cato,* written by Joseph Addison in 1713, was a favorite of Washington for obvious reasons. Cato was a young Roman who challenged Julius Caesar and wanted Rome to remain a republic. When the play opens, Cato's army is outnumbered and the soldiers await Caesar's attack. "What pity is it that we can die but once to serve our country," Cato says. These lines from the play may have been the source of the words traditionally believed to have been spoken by Captain Nathan Hale of the Continental Army in 1776 when he was about to be hanged by the British as a spy: "I only regret that I have but one life to lose for my country."

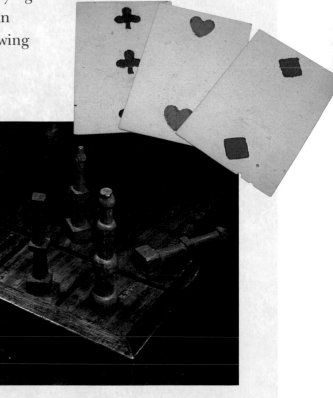

All was not grim and gloomy at Valley Forge, where a soldier whittled these chessmen, which saw action during off-duty hours. Playing cards and gambling were forbidden. But many a knapsack still contained a deck of cards.

In a scene imagined by the artist, a flag is hoisted at Valley Forge. Congress did adopt a 13-star, 13-stripe flag on June 14, 1777, but there is no record that such a flag was flown at Valley Forge.

Valley Forge, chosen as winter quarters, had become a place where the soldiers lingered into spring, a time of new birth, forging a new army. On May 1, the camp celebrated May Day with a pageant and "mirth and jollity." Soldiers put dogwood blossoms in their hats and paraded behind fifers and drummers from one Maypole to another. Five days later, the Continental Army celebrated the news that the king of France had agreed to help the Americans by sending troops and munitions. The decision had been made in February, but Washington waited to tell his men until he had received official word from Congress.

Cannon boomed salutes and thousands of soldiers performed a *feu de joie*, a fire of joy, by shooting muskets one after the other in a running fire. Muskets cracked and flashed up and down the ranks in a stunning display of the united army that Washington had envisioned and von Steuben had produced.

Washington had won the loyalty of his men, but he still had to deal with Congress. Back in January 1778, a congressional committee had arrived in Valley Forge to inspect the Continental Army and talk to Washington about his plans. He had focused on the need to retain his officers through better pay and the promise of a pension (pay on retirement). Congress eventually agreed, and in spring the resignations stopped. Congress also displayed its power—and its awareness of Tory recruitment temptations, such as promises of land grants—by ordering Continental Army officers to declare their loyalty.

They had to swear their loyalty to the United States and renounce George III, his heirs, and anyone who aided the king. General Washington handed out small pieces of paper with the "Oath of Allegiance" printed on them. Each officer at Valley Forge, including Washington, placed his hand upon a Bible, swore the oath, then filled in his name and rank and signed the paper. Among the officers who signed was Major General Benedict Arnold, the wounded hero of the battle of Saratoga, who had arrived at Valley Forge with other veterans of the fighting in New York.

Washington could walk among his men and see a trained and proud army. But he had another worry: smallpox. Epidemics of the dreaded disease had been sweeping through the American colonies for decades.

In 1751, 19-year-old George Washington had accompanied his older half-brother Lawrence to Barbados, a British possession in the Caribbean. Lawrence was hoping, in vain, that the warm climate would cure his tuberculosis. While there, George Washington caught smallpox, a highly contagious, often fatal disease that left permanent pits or scars on the victims who survived. George suffered through a high fever, aches all over his body, and an outbreak of pus-filled, blister-like pimples called pustules. Luckily, he survived. Unlike typical victims whose bodies bear numerous scars and pockmarks, he had only a few scars on his nose.

Survivors could not get smallpox again; they were immune. This fact led to the idea of *ingrafting* (later called inoculation): making a small cut in a person's arm and putting bits of a pustule into the cut to produce a mild case of smallpox.

A year after Major General Benedict Arnold signed this loyalty oath at Valley Forge, he turned traitor, contacting a British spy with an offer to sell secrets.

Most people suffered for weeks but then became immune. By the 18th century, inoculation was well known in America. John and Abigail Adams and their children had been inoculated, as had Martha Washington, her children, and everyone at Washington's Mount Vernon estate, including the slaves.

When Washington assumed command of the Continental Army, he ordered inoculations for every soldier and officer. Soon after arriving in Valley Forge he learned that between 3,000 and 4,000 men, mostly new recruits, had not been inoculated when they enlisted. (Private Joseph Plumb Martin had been. He had spent 16 days recovering and "broke out all over with boils," some "big as half a hen's egg.")

Washington's insistence on an army free of smallpox meant that he had to put many of his already weakened men through the torment of the inoculation treatment. In May 1778, nearly 3,800 men were unfit for duty. They included

Washington visits a wounded soldier. He was probably shot or bayoneted by British soldiers during a clash in the countryside around Valley Forge. Both armies sent out patrols whose mission was to find food or stop the enemy from finding food. Many sick or wounded men were sent to hospitals elsewhere in Pennsylvania.

"Men in the Small Pox or under innoculations." Washington tried to keep his smallpox war secret, because the British Army might strike if their spies learned how many men were laid low by inoculations.

Both sides were using spies in hopes of finding out what spring would bring. Washington's agents in Philadelphia learned that the British, reacting to the French alliance with America, had ordered General Howe back to England and were replacing him with General Sir Henry Clinton, who knew America better than Howe did. Clinton had served in the New York militia when his father was royal governor of the colony. He had fought the Americans at Bunker Hill and in the battle of Long Island, where he had earned a knighthood. What would he do when he arrived in Philadelphia? Would he stay or lead the British out of the city? Would he attack Valley Forge? While Washington asked himself these questions, word came to Valley Forge about a farewell party being planned for General Howe. There would also be a surprise for Howe planned by General Washington.

Washington points to supply wagons arriving on a spring day. His men cheer and even cartwheel. Seeking food from area farmers, supply officers advertised in a local newspaper for "Fresh Pork, Fat Turkey, Goose, Rough skinned Potatoes, Turnips, Indian Meal, Sour-Crout, Leaf Tobacco, New Milk, Cyder, and Small [low-alcohol] Beer."

Washington charges into battle at Monmouth Court House, New Jersey. Brandishing his sword, he leads his men out of the confusion caused by the retreat ordered by Major General Charles Lee, who slumps on his white horse at left.

the road to victory

On the afternoon of May 18, 1778, two days before General Clinton took over as Howe's replacement, British officers and their Tory friends began a daylong going-away party for General Howe. The party's organizer was Howe's aide, Captain John André. He called his creation the *Mischianza,* meaning "medley" or "mixture" in Italian, one of the four languages that the dashing André spoke. The spectacle, so oddly out of place in the middle of a war, showed the way Howe's casual manner toward combat had spread to his officers.

While von Steuben had been showing Washington's officers how to build an army, Howe's officers had spent most of their time amusing themselves by staging plays, dances, and parties. They failed to see that by attacking Valley Forge they probably could have won the war. But nothing they did in their idle hours compared to the Mischianza and what a Quaker called its "Scenes of folly and vanity." The festivities began with the boom of cannon salutes as a fleet of "Galleys, Barges, & flat boats, finely decorated" and carrying officers and their ladies slowly moved down the Delaware River, while shipboard bands played "God Save the King."

The partygoers left their vessels at a landing and walked between ranks of soldiers and lines of mounted British dragoons. The walk ended at a large square of lawn flanked by triumphal arches and grandstands, where the ladies and officers sat. In each of the front rows were seven beautiful young women wearing flowing, Turkish-style gowns and jeweled turbans. One of them was probably Peggy Shippen, who would later become Mrs. Benedict Arnold and play an important role in her husband's decision to betray the cause to which he had sworn allegiance at Valley Forge.

Launching the dramatic events of the Mischianza was a reenactment of a medieval joust between two bands of knights on horseback. After the jousting, the revelers walked to a nearby mansion and danced in a glittering ballroom.

This ticket admitted partygoers to the Mischianza, *a farewell gala for General William Howe. Translated, the Latin banner hails him: "He shines as he sets, but he shall rise again in great splendor."*

Make-believe knights, preparing to joust, salute turbaned ladies at the spectacular Mischianza, organized by Captain John André, who would soon produce a spy plot starring Benedict Arnold. About 20 British officers chipped in to pay for the lavish party for General Howe.

At ten o'clock, all stood at the windows and gasped at a fireworks display taking place along the riverfront. At midnight, "large folding-doors, hitherto artfully concealed" suddenly opened and revealed a huge dining hall built by British Army engineers as a temporary addition to the mansion. Bowing before the 430 guests were "twenty-four black slaves in Oriental dresses, with silver collars and bracelets."

Suddenly, on the grounds outside there was a rattle of gunfire and a flare of flame. Guests were told that this was all part of the celebration. But the truth was that under Washington's orders some dragoons from Valley Forge were staging their own Mischianza. While nearly everyone in the city had been preoccupied with the festivities, the cavalry had sneaked to nearby redoubts, poured whale oil over timber barricades, and set them afire. Sentries fired at them, but they all escaped. The daring raid began a clash that would test a young French general and the new Continental Army.

Washington, believing that Howe would make one last move before Clinton took command, had ordered a bold countermove as a farewell surprise for Howe. A strong reconnaissance, or scouting, force of 2,200 men was to leave Valley Forge and probe the British defenses around Philadelphia to see what was stirring. The raid on the Mischianza was a stab by an advance dragoon unit—part of the scouting force—led by Major General the Marquis de Lafayette.

Lafayette had in his force 50 men armed with long rifles—sometimes called the secret weapon of the Revolution. The inner surface of the rifle barrel had spiral grooves that spun the ball-shaped bullet as it sped down the barrel. The spinning gave the rifle ball far more accuracy and a longer range than a musket ball. A skilled rifleman could kill a foe 400 yards away. The long rifle—also called the American, Kentucky, or Pennsylvania rifle—was originally made by German-American gunsmiths in Pennsylvania. The barrel was usually about 4 feet long. Riflemen typically wore broad-brimmed round hats and fringed, loose-fitting "rifle shirts" that gave them easier arm movements than jackets did. Also with Lafayette were 47 Oneida Indians whom he had recruited on a mission to New York. The Oneidas, among the few native nations who fought on the American side, were armed with muskets.

Soon after Lafayette's force set up camp at Barren Hill (now Lafayette Hill), five miles west of Philadelphia, a deserter made his way to British lines and, offering his services as a spy, reported the location of the Americans.

The "eating, drinking, dancing, etc." at the Mischianza "was concluded about Seven the next morning," a British officer remembered. Then, soberly, he added that some celebrants "think it ill-timed." He may have been referring to the fact that even as celebrants were staggering home that morning, the guest of honor, General Howe, decided to go back to work. Determined to capture Lafayette, Howe sent out some 6,000 troops in a maneuver designed to encircle the young French general's troops.

This Continental Army soldier wears the outfit of a rifleman: loose-fitting linen hunting shirt, Indian-like leggings and moccasins.

But Lafayette had ordered the riflemen and the Oneidas to guard the road to Philadelphia. When the British advance unit came up that road, muskets and accurate rifle fire stopped them. This gave Lafayette's troops enough time to retreat, wading across a Schuylkill River ford.

By the time the Redcoats reached Barren Hill and headed for the Schuylkill, most of Lafayette's men were across and on their way back to Valley Forge. The riflemen and the Oneidas made a stand at the river and drove off the British, who returned to Philadelphia. Lafayette's men, so recently schooled by von Steuben in the art of maneuvering, had escaped the British trap and had survived the first real test of what they had learned. Back in Valley Forge, they prepared for the end of winter quarters and the start of a new season of war for Washington's new army.

Two days after Lafayette's daring raid, Howe called in some Tory officials and told them to make peace with the rebels in the city because the British Army would soon leave Philadelphia. That day came on June 18, when General Clinton led the British out of Philadelphia.

Washington, with his strengthened and disciplined army, was ready.

Clinton's superiors in London, believing that America's French allies might attack New York, had ordered him to leave for that city by sea. But frightened Philadelphia Tories begged to be taken to the Tory stronghold of New York, along with the British Army. The Tories did not want to face their Patriot neighbors after the British left. Clinton decided he would take his troops to New York by land so that the Tories—about 3,000 men, women, and children—could flee on British ships. A woman wrote of seeing carts and wagons, "laden with dry goods and household furniture, dragged through the streets by men to the wharves for want of horses." Royal Navy sailors threw many of the possessions overboard to make room for military supplies. A shortage of horses was caused by Clinton's decision to rescue the Tories. Supplies and ammunition that he would have loaded on ships now had to be moved overland. He needed more than 1,500 horse-drawn wagons. To protect the wagons, he put some of his men in front of the wagon train and some behind

it, making the British line of march about 12 miles long. In one of those wagons were books, musical instruments, and other loot taken by Captain André from the home of Ben Franklin, where André had lived during the occupation of the city.

On June 19, when Washington was convinced that the last of the British troops—now about 14,000 men strong—were across the Delaware River, he started marching his army out of Valley Forge in pursuit. Around sundown that day, a small force under Major General Benedict Arnold entered Philadelphia. Washington had given Arnold, one of his most trusted generals, a difficult task. Congress, still in York and getting ready to return to Philadelphia, had passed a resolution forbidding any revenge against Tories and others who had aided the British. Arnold declared martial law, meaning that he ruled over the city like a dictator.

Ever since the British had left Philadelphia, New Jersey militiamen had been shadowing them, sending information back to Washington. By June 26

British troops, accompanied by civilian stragglers known as camp followers, head for New Jersey after leaving Philadelphia with Washington in pursuit. Exactly six months after the Americans entered Valley Forge, the Continental Army marched out, transformed from a dispirited, ragged band to a strong and disciplined army.

the British had reached Monmouth Court House (now Freehold), New Jersey, about 35 miles from ships waiting to ferry the troops and supplies from New Jersey across New York Bay to New York City.

The British troops camped around a road flanked by ravines and leading across a bridge to a stretch of swampy land. Beyond were high grounds and a better road that would speed up the march to the ships.

Washington ordered Major General Charles Lee to pounce on the British rear guard when the troops left camp on June 28, splitting that part of the army off from the rest of Clinton's men. Washington would then hurl his main force at the forward section of the British. Amid clouds of dust under a murderous sun, scattered units of British and American forces were spread across a battlefield that covered some 20 miles. Soldiers on both sides dropped from heat exhaustion.

A legend is born on the Monmouth Court House battlefield: "Molly Pitcher" replaces her fallen husband at the cannon he had manned. Some sources identify her as the wife of artillery-man William Hayes. She is said to have earned her nickname by carrying pitchers of water to numerous gunners and their smoking guns.

There was no attack. Lee failed to fight. Instead, he ordered a retreat.

An infuriated Washington rode up to Lee. Private Martin was standing close enough to Washington to hear words that sounded very much like swearing. "Very unlike him," Martin thought, but Washington "seemed at the instant to be in a great passion."

"What is the meaning of this?" an angry Washington asked Lee. "What is all this confusion for? This retreat?"

While Lee sputtered an answer, Washington gathered Lafayette and other officers around him and started calmly giving orders. Martin saw British cannon shells "rending up the earth all around" Washington. When the bewildered retreating soldiers were asked if they could fight, they answered Washington with three cheers. "His presence stopped the retreat," Lafayette later wrote.

The retreating troops turned around and formed precise musket lines. Von Steuben, helping to round up the scattered troops, must have been proud. Washington, riding along the lines under fire, once again used his skill for seeing terrain, spotting ridges and hills where he ordered the positioning of infantrymen, dragoons, and cannon. At one of the cannon, Martin saw a woman helping her husband, an artilleryman. While "in the act of reaching a cartridge and having one of her feet as far before the other as she could step, a cannon shot from the enemy passed directly between her legs" and carried away part of her petticoat. She kept on working at the cannon. Another account tells of Mary Hayes, the wife of a Pennsylvania artilleryman, who joined her husband's cannon crew on the battlefield. From such stories came the legend of Molly Pitcher.

Washington's attack drove back the British rear guard. The battle ended with both Americans and British settling down for a night of rest. Before dawn, Clinton ordered the rejoining of the rear unit, the wagon train, and the rest of his troops, and the reconnected army slipped away on the high road. Although the British successfully escaped, the closely fought battle proved that the Continental Army that marched out of Valley Forge was strong enough and disciplined enough to stand and fight the finest troops of the British Army.

After the battle of Monmouth Court House and a subsequent battle at Springfield, New Jersey, British strategy focused on splitting the Colonies by invading the South. The British expected to get military help by recruiting thousands of southern Tories. Many did support the British, aiding Lord General Charles Cornwallis, commander of British forces in the South. The British seemed to have the southern colonies in their grasp until General Washington sent Major General Greene, along with soldiers trained at Valley Forge, to the South. Greene's decisive action at Guilford Courthouse blunted the British invasion of North Carolina and drove Cornwallis into Virginia.

Cornwallis, desperately in need of supplies, headed for the port of Yorktown, Virginia, where, he confidently believed, the Royal Navy would deliver him what he needed. But in September 1781, a French fleet intercepted and battered the British warships off Virginia, sending them back to New York under tattered sails. The French victory doomed Cornwallis, who could not be supplied from the sea. On September 28, American and French troops began a siege of Cornwallis's troops, gradually tightening the grip.

"We had come a long way to see them," Private Martin said in his recollection of the long march to trap the British at Yorktown.

A temporary shortage of food at Yorktown sent Martin's memory drifting back to Valley Forge and "our old associate, Hunger." Days passed as he and his American and French comrades continued the siege. Finally, on October 19, Cornwallis, realizing that he had no escape by land or sea, surrendered. Martin and many other veterans of Valley Forge watched as the surrendering British Army "marched to the place appointed and stacked their arms."

The war was nearly over. No more major battles would be fought. But not until 1783 would the peace treaty be signed. The war lasted eight long years, and its history is usually told by telling of its battles. What happened at Valley Forge was not a battle, but about 1,700 men did die during winter quarters there, some killed by hunger, disease, or cold, and some killed in skirmishes by British guns or bayonets.

Valley Forge was a battlefield where thousands of ragged, starving men were made into an army. And Valley Forge was a battlefield where men fought winter and neglect, using courage and faith as their weapons. George Washington put it this way: "To see Men without Cloathes to cover their nakedness, without Blankets to lay on, without Shoes, by which their Marches might be traced by the Blood from their feet, and almost as often without Provisions as with. . .without a House. . .to cover them. . .is a mark of patience and obedience which in my opinion can scarce be parallel'd."

Valley Forge was also a battlefield where General George Washington had to fight politicians and plotters, pitting his integrity and devotion to duty against the fears and ignorance of men far from the hunger and despair of Valley Forge. It was indeed a forge, where suffering and discipline hammered a band of brave men, turning them into an army with a new spirit and resolve. Without the victory over hardship, without the new army that marched out of winter and into spring at Valley Forge, the Revolution almost certainly would have been lost.

British troops surrender at Yorktown, Virginia, on October 19, 1781, all but ending the Revolutionary War. General Lord Charles Cornwallis, commander of British forces in the South, did not want to surrender in person. He sent General Charles O'Hara, shown here surrendering his sword to Major General Benjamin Lincoln, who represented George Washington.

NAKED AND STARVING AS THEY ARE
WE CANNOT ENOUGH ADMIRE
THE INCOMPARABLE PATIENCE AND FIDELITY
OF THE SOLDIERY

56

The National Memorial Arch towers over Valley Forge.
With a design based on Roman triumphal arches, it honors
General George Washington and the men of his victorious
Continental Army. The arch was dedicated in 1917.

By the spring of 1779, the Valley Forge of huts and hunger was beginning to fade away. Farmers started tearing down the huts and using the logs for firewood or fences. The site continued to serve the Continental Army, first as a hospital camp, then as an ordnance depot, a prisoner of war camp, and a musket factory.

In September 1781, American Lieutenant Enos Reeves, on his way to Philadelphia, wandered into Valley Forge. "We. . .came thro' our old Encampment, or rather the first huts of the whole army," he wrote. "Some of officers' huts are inhabited, but the greater part are decayed, some are split up into rails, and a number of fine fields are to be seen on the level ground that was cleared, but in places where they have let the shoots grow, it is already like a half grown young wood."

In 1850 the son of a Revolutionary War veteran told a story about his father: He was plowing a field at Valley Forge one day when an elderly man rode up, dismounted from his horse, and began asking questions about farming in the area. The stranger identified himself as a Virginia planter named George Washington. The family story may well be true, for, according to Washington's diaries, he did make a fishing trip to Valley Forge in 1787, while taking a break from presiding over the Constitutional Convention in Philadelphia. His diaries also mention farming practices in the area, perhaps based on his talks with local farmers.

The land where Washington's army camped became a park operated by a state commission. Park officials often squabbled over land purchases and questions of historical accuracy. In 1936, Pennsylvania's Governor Earle, responding to a dispute over the sale of hot dogs on this "sacred soil," declared that the soldiers "who wintered at Valley Forge would have been thankful had they had an abundant supply of 'hot dogs.'"

Valley Forge became an official national historical site in 1977, when responsibility passed to the National Park Service. It is maintained as a shrine, where an army was reborn and where George Washington began his journey from defeated general to a hero hailed by a new nation.

General George Washington of Valley Forge would go on to become the first president of the nation he had helped to found. And when Washington died in 1799, it would be a cavalryman who fought at Valley Forge, Captain Henry Lee—"Light Horse Harry Lee"—who would write words that so perfectly described Washington: "first in war, first in peace, and first in the hearts of his countrymen."

TIME LINE OF THE REVOLUTIONARY WAR

The Revolutionary War traces back to the French and Indian War, which started with skirmishes in 1754 and ended in 1763. George Washington was one of the thousands of Americans who fought on the king's side and triumphed over the French troops and their Indian allies.

Colonists had been pushing westward across the Appalachian Mountains. In 1763, King George III tried to stop this migration with his Proclamation Line (see map). Then came new taxes, ordered by the British Parliament to help pay the enormous cost of the war.

Incidents increased between British authorities and Americans who denounced Parliament and cried out against "taxation without representation," After these Patriots dumped tea into Boston Harbor in 1773, the king closed the harbor and replaced Massachusetts's royal governor with a general. Tories, people loyal to the king, hoped for peace, while Patriots armed themselves with muskets they had carried for the king a decade before. These veterans and others from Maine to Georgia would go to war again. This time, they would fight the king.

1763
King George III proclaims that all land west of the Allegheny Mountains is reserved for Indians, thus barring colonists from migrating to western lands.

1764
The British Parliament passes the Sugar Act, which increases not only taxes in the Colonies but also the powers of royal officials to enforce the taxes.

1765
Parliament passes the Billeting Act, which requires colonists to provide housing and supplies for British soldiers sent to the Colonies, and the Stamp Act, which requires every piece of printed paper to have a special stamp attached.

Rebellious colonists form the Sons of Liberty, an anti-British underground organization, and Committees of Correspondence help keep the Colonies in touch. Representatives from nine Colonies, meeting at the Stamp Act Congress in New York City, vote to send the king and Parliament a Declaration of Rights and Grievances.

1766
Stunned by the reaction to the stamp tax, Parliament repeals it.

1767
Parliament passes what become known as the Townshend Acts—taxes on imported items such as paper, paint, glass, and tea. Colonists, including women who became known as Daughters of Liberty, boycott all British goods.

1768
British customs (tax) officials in Boston, cracking down on smugglers, seize the merchant ship *Liberty,* owned by rebel leader John Hancock. Rioting erupts and colonists get a phrase to explain their anger at a distant government: "No taxation without representation." British troops arrive in Boston to maintain order.

1770
Under pressure from British manufacturers, Parliament repeals all the Townshend taxes except the one on tea. A Boston mob taunts jittery British soldiers, who fire at the crowd, killing five. The "Boston Massacre" ignites anti-British sentiment throughout New England.

1772
Patriots in Rhode Island board the *Gaspee,* a grounded British warship that had been on anti-smuggling patrol. They wound the Royal Navy captain and set fire to the ship. All escape as news of this daring act spreads through the Colonies.

1773
Britain decides to enforce the tea tax and sell tea through its own agents. Many merchants join the rebels. Urged on by Samuel Adams, Patriots disguised as Indians board three British ships, break open boxes of tea, and dump it into Boston Harbor.

1774
King George and Parliament react to the "Boston Tea Party" by closing the harbor until the dumped tea is paid for. Other "Intolerable Acts" give royal officials control of the Massachusetts legislature, outlaw Boston town meetings, and order the transfer of some criminal trials to England. Colonies send delegates to the First Continental Congress in Philadelphia. State militias, preparing for war, organize rapid-response units called minutemen.

1775
British soldiers march from Boston to nearby Concord to seize gunpowder stored by Patriots. Paul Revere and William Dawes ride to warn rebels and muster minutemen.

British and rebels clash at Lexington, then at Concord, in the first battles of the American Revolution.

Militiamen begin to arrive in Boston from the other Colonies. Vermont's Green Mountain Boys, led by Ethan Allen and Benedict Arnold, capture Fort Ticonderoga, New York.

As the Patriots begin a siege of Boston, fierce fighting flares on Breed's Hill in a battle that takes its name from nearby Bunker Hill. Tories (Loyalists) denounce the Revolution. Many take up arms and join the British side.

In Philadelphia, the Second Continental Congress names George Washington commander in chief of the armed force assembling in Boston and declares that it is the Continental Army.

In an "Olive Branch Petition" to King George, the Continental Congress claims colonists'

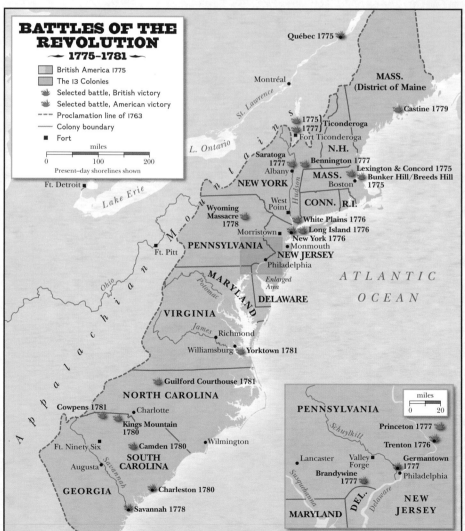

BATTLES OF THE REVOLUTION
1775–1781

- British America 1775
- The 13 Colonies
- Selected battle, British victory
- Selected battle, American victory
- - - Proclamation line of 1763
- — Colony boundary
- ■ Fort

miles
0   100   200
Present–day shorelines shown

Québec 1775

Montréal

St. Lawrence

L. Ontario

MASS.
(District of Maine)

Castine 1779

1775
1777 Ticonderoga
Fort Ticonderoga

N.H.

Saratoga 1777
Albany
Bennington 1777
Lexington & Concord 1775
Bunker Hill/Breeds Hill 1775
MASS.
Boston

NEW YORK

West Point

CONN.   R.I.

Ft. Detroit

Lake Erie

Wyoming Massacre 1778

Morristown
White Plains 1776
Long Island 1776
New York 1776
Monmouth

Hudson

PENNSYLVANIA

Ft. Pitt

Ohio

MARYLAND

Philadelphia

Enlarged Area

DELAWARE

ATLANTIC OCEAN

Potomac

VIRGINIA

James   Richmond

Williamsburg   Yorktown 1781

Guilford Courthouse 1781

NORTH CAROLINA

Cowpens 1781   Charlotte

Kings Mountain 1780

Ft. Ninety Six   Camden 1780   Wilmington

SOUTH CAROLINA

Augusta   Savannah

GEORGIA

Charleston 1780

Savannah 1778

Appalachian Mountains

(Inset map)

miles
0   20

PENNSYLVANIA

Schuylkill

Princeton 1777

Trenton 1776

Lancaster   Valley Forge

Germantown 1777

Brandywine 1777   Philadelphia

Susquehanna

MARYLAND   DEL.   Delaware

NEW JERSEY

rights as loyal subjects. The king refuses to read the petition and declares the colonists in "open and avowed rebellion."

Americans invade Canada and take Montréal, but they are defeated at Québec.

Lord Dunmore, royal governor of Virginia, offers freedom to slaves who join the British. Hundreds of slaves leave their masters. Dunmore forms the Ethiopian Regiment.

1776
British troops evacuate Boston and sail to Halifax, Canada, taking with them about 1,000 Loyalists.

The Continental Congress passes the Declaration of Independence, which says "these United Colonies are, and of Right ought to be Free and Independent States."

British General William Howe leads 9,300 British soldiers who land on Staten Island in the first British move to take New York City.

In the Battle of Long Island, Howe defeats George Washington, whose force escapes to New York. The British hang an American officer, Nathan Hale, for spying. British troops take New York City, which they will occupy throughout the war. Tories, fleeing from Patriots in Connecticut and elsewhere, flock to New York.

The British occupy Newport, Rhode Island.

Thomas Paine's "The Crisis," Number One—"These are the times that try men's souls"—is published in Philadelphia.

In a daring Christmas attack at Trenton, New Jersey, George Washington's troops defeat the Hessians, Britain's hired German soldiers.

1777
Washington begins the year with a victory at Princeton, New Jersey.

The Marquis de Lafayette of France arrives in Philadelphia and is commissioned a major general in the Continental Army.

Washington's army, defeated at Brandywine and Germantown, fails to keep the British from taking Philadelphia (see Road to Valley Forge, below).

British General John Burgoyne, defeated in battles centered at Saratoga, New York, surrenders his 5,871 men to General Horatio Gates. The victory helps to convince France to aid the American cause.

The Continental Congress, meeting in York, Pennsylvania, creates the Articles of Confederation as the basis for governing the United States of America. The Articles are ratified by the states and take effect on March 1, 1781.

King Louis XVI of France accepts American independence, opening the way for France to openly aid the United States.

1778
Rhode Island enlists slaves to form an all-black regiment commanded by a white officer.

Washington's army attacks the British at Monmouth Court House, New Jersey.

Beginning hit-and-run attacks along the New York and Pennsylvania frontier, Loyalists and their Indian allies invade the Wyoming Valley.

The British begin a southern campaign by invading Georgia and recruiting Tories. Savannah falls to British control.

1779
British conquer Augusta, Georgia. Americans pull back to Charleston, South Carolina.

Spain declares war on Britain.

To drive British forces from the Castine Peninsula in Penobscot Bay, Maine, Americans mount the largest amphibious operation of the war. The Americans suffer a disastrous defeat. Paul Revere, one of the leaders, gets much of the blame.

John Paul Jones, captain of the *Bonhomme Richard,* attacks towns and shipping along the English coast. In a battle against the Royal Navy's *Serapis,* with his ship burning and sinking, Jones is told to surrender. He shouts, "I have not yet begun to fight." The *Serapis* surrenders and Jones sails her to France.

Major General Benedict Arnold becomes a spy for the British.

The British evacuate Rhode Island.

New York declares 59 Tories outlaws and seizes their property.

1780
Charleston falls to the British.

French forces land at Newport, Rhode Island, and soon will be fighting alongside Americans.

Major General Benedict Arnold, commander of West Point, the vital Hudson River fort, betrays his country, giving fort plans to the British spymaster, Major John André. Learning that André had been captured, Arnold flees to a waiting British ship. He becomes a brigadier general in the British Army.

Lieutenant General Charles Earl Cornwallis, commanding British southern troops, gains control of Georgia and South Carolina after defeating Major General Horatio Gates at Camden, South Carolina.

John André is hanged as a spy.

Guerrilla warfare breaks out in the Carolinas, with Tories fighting Patriots. In the ferocious battle of Kings Mountain, near the South Carolina-North Carolina border,

backwoodsmen from the Carolinas, Georgia, Virginia, and present-day Tennessee, defeat a Tory force led by a British officer—the only non-American on the battlefield.

1781
Major General Nathanael Greene, commander of America's southern army, brilliantly outmaneuvers Cornwallis. Americans win the Battle of Cowpens in South Carolina. Then, at Guilford Courthouse, North Carolina, he finds Cornwallis, riddles his ranks (532 British casualties; 261 American), and withdraws. With the British holding only Charleston and Savannah in the South, Cornwallis heads for Virginia.

General Washington and Lieutenant General Comte de Rochambeau lead a combined American-French force on a march from New York through Virginia, from Williamsburg to Yorktown, where Cornwallis's army is encamped.

A French fleet under Admiral Comte de Grasse drives off a British fleet that Cornwallis expected to supply him.

Under siege and outnumbered, Cornwallis surrenders on October 19. The Revolutionary War is all but over.

1782
Benjamin Franklin, John Adams, John Jay, and Henry Laurens begin negotiating a peace treaty in Paris, France.

1783
The Treaty of Paris is signed, officially ending the war. The last British troops on American soil evacuate New York City.

Thousands of Tories, including ex-slaves, sail to Nova Scotia in fleets of British ships. Given land and supplies by Britain, they begin colonizing Canada.

Road to Valley Forge

1777
July
General Howe loads about 15,000 men aboard warships under command of his brother, Admiral Lord Richard Howe, and sails from New York.

August
Howe lands his men, many of them sick, at Head of Elk, Maryland, about 50 miles southwest of Philadelphia.

Washington moves his troops to block Howe's advance to Philadelphia.

September
Howe outmaneuvers

Washington in a battle at Brandywine, near Philadelphia.

Congress flees Philadelphia, going to Lancaster, then York.

October
British troops enter Philadelphia and are welcomed by Loyalists.

At Germantown, Pennsylvania, British again are victorious.

November
Washington encamps at Whitemarsh, north of Philadelphia.

December
Americans and British skirmish around Whitemarsh. General Howe withdraws to the comfort of the former American capital.

Washington leads his starving, ragged army to Valley Forge.

1778
March
Baron von Steuben begins training American troops at Valley Forge.

May
France officially becomes an American ally, leading to the British withdrawal from Philadelphia. General Sir Henry Clinton replaces General Howe.

June
Washington's strengthened, well-trained army leaves Valley Forge and pursues the British as they head for New York City, fighting them at Monmouth, NJ.

selected sources

Adams, John: Letter from John Adams to Abigail Adams, 26 October 1777. Adams Family Papers: An Electronic Archive at http://www.masshist.org/digitaladams/

Bancroft, George. *A History of the United States, From the Discovery of the American Continent.* Boston: Little, Brown and Co, 1834.

Bodle, Wayne. *Valley Forge Winter.* University Park, PA: Pennsylvania State University Press, 2002.

Brandt, Clare. *The Man in the Mirror: A Life of Benedict Arnold.* New York: Random House, 1994.

Buchanan, John. *The Road to Valley Forge.* New York: Wiley, 2004.

Ellis, Joseph J. *His Excellency George Washington.* New York: Knopf, 2004.

Ewing, George. *Journal of George Ewing.* The 54-page journal is published at http://www.sandcastles.net/george.htm on a Web site devoted to the Ewing family.

Ferling, Joseph E. "Joseph Galloway, a Reassessment of a Pennsylvania Loyalist," *Pennsylvania History* (39 [2]) 1972.

Fiske, John. T*he American Revolution, Vol. 2.* Boston: Houghton Mifflin, 1891.

Fleming, Thomas. *Washington's Secret War.* New York: HarperCollins/Smithsonian Books, 2005.

Flexner, James Thomas. *Washington, the Indispensable Man.* Boston: Little, Brown, 1974.

Golway, Terry. *Washington's General.* New York: Henry Holt, 2005.

Ketchum, Richard M. *The Winter Soldiers.* New York: Doubleday, 1973.

Lossing, Benson J. *Pictorial Field Book of the Revolution, Volume II* at http://freepages.history.rootsweb.com/~wcarr1/Lossing1/Chap37.html

Marshall, John. *The Life of George Washington* at http://www.gutenberg.org/etext/18593.

Martin, Joseph Plumb. *A Narrative of a Revolutionary Soldier.* New York: Signet Classic, 2001.

McCullough, David. *1776.* New York: Simon & Schuster, 2005.

Paine, Thomas. "The Crisis." Reprinted at http://www.ushistory.org/paine/crisis/index.htm

Peterson, Harold L. *The Book of the Continental Soldier.* Harrisburg, PA: Stackpole, 1968.

Royster, Charles. *A Revolutionary People at War.* Chapel Hill, NC: University of North Carolina Press, 1979.

Showman, Richard K., editor. *The Papers of General Nathanael Greene.* Chapel Hill, NC: University of North Carolina Press, 1976.

Smith, Page. *A New Age Now Begins, Vol. 2.* New York: McGraw-Hill, 1976.

Steuben, Friedrich Wilhelm von. *Revolutionary War Drill Manual.* New York, Dover, 1985 (facsimile reprint of 1794 edition).

Tallmadge, Benjamin. *Memoir of Colonel Benjamin Tallmadge.* New York, 1958. Reprinted. New York: New York Times & Arno Press, 1968.

Thompson, Henry F. "A Letter of Miss Rebecca Franks, 1778," *Pennsylvania Magazine of History and Biography,* Vol. 16.

Treese, Lorett. *Valley Forge: Making and Remaking a National Symbol.* University Park, PA: Pennsylvania State University Press, 1995.

Trussell, John B. *Birthplace of an Army.* Harrisburg, PA: Pennsylvania Historical and Museum Commission, 1998.

Waldo, Albigence: "Diary of Surgeon Albigence Waldo," at http://odur.let.rug.nl/%7Eusa/D/1776-1800/war/waldo.htm

quote sources

Quotations from George Washington come from *The Writings of George Washington from the Original Manuscript Sources, 1745–1799.* These volumes, edited by John C. Fitzpatrick and published by the U.S. Government Printing Office in 1931, can be found on the Internet at http://etext.virginia.edu/washington/fitzpatrick/. At that site you can search through the 39 volumes by words or phrases.

Numbers in bold refer to pages in this book where a quote is found, followed by the name of the speaker, the source identified by author's last name, as indicated in the Selected Sources above. If a published source, the page is given; if the publication is reprinted on the Internet, the quote can be found by a search of that site.

11 Paine. **12** Rawdon: McCullough, 251. **15** Greenwood: McCullough, 277. **17** Martin: Martin, 61. Howe: Bancroft, 245. **19** Duer: Bodle, 57. Martin: Martin, 88. **21** Supply officer: Bodle, 51. **22** Waldo: Waldo, Dec. 14, 1777. **24** Smith, 998. **25–26** Martin: Martin, 88–89. **29** Tallmadge: Tallmadge, December 1777. Galloway: Ferling, 165, 178. **30–31** Adams: Adams, October 26, 1777. **31** Conway: Lossing, footnote 25, Chapter 5. **32** Waldo: Waldo, December 21, 1777. **34** Greene: Showman (Greene to Clement Biddle) February 14, 1778, Vol. 2, p. 283. **35** Franks: Thompson, 216. **37** Waldo: Waldo, December 28, 1777. Paine: Paine. **38** Franklin: Steuben, "Publisher's Note." von Steuben: Steuben, 11. **39** Ewing: Ewing, 34. **40** Martin: Martin, 102–103. **41** Ewing: Ewing, 35. **44** Martin: Martin, 57–58. **48–49** Mischianza: Lossing (John André description, endnote to Vol. II, Chapter 4). **53** Martin: Martin, 111 (quoting Washington). Lafayette: Marshall, Vol. 3, Chapter 1, footnote 8. Martin: Martin, 115. **54** Martin: Martin, 197, 207. **57** Reeves: Treese, 4. Earle: Treese, 117.

selected postscripts

John André became spymaster for General Sir Henry Clinton when he arrived in New York. André used his newly married Philadelphia friend, Peggy Shippen Arnold, to reach her husband, who had offered to spy for the British. André, caught after getting secrets from Arnold, was tried and hanged.

Benedict Arnold, while military governor of Philadelphia, fell in love with Peggy Shippen—and with wealth. In April 1779, when he was 37 years old and Peggy was 19, they were married. Aided by a Tory, Arnold contacted John André, British spymaster in New York, and offered to sell secrets. In September 1780, while Arnold was commander of West Point, a key fort on the Hudson River, he gave André drawings of the fort's defenses. André was caught; Arnold escaped. Then, as a British general, he led Tory soldiers in battle against fellow Americans. In 1781, Arnold and Peggy sailed to England. He died there in 1801.

Peggy Shippen Arnold helped her husband and John André in the spy plot that ended in André's execution. In exile in England and in Nova Scotia, she stuck by Arnold, father of her four children. In 1790, she made a brief visit to Philadelphia, where she was treated with "much coldness and neglect." Arnold died owing a great deal of money. Peggy paid off his debts "down to the last teaspoon" before she died in 1804.

Nathanael Greene, as commander of the Continental Army's Southern Department, in 1781, drove the British out of the interior of the Carolinas and Georgia and made the American-French war-winning victory at Yorktown, Virginia, possible. Presented tracts of southern land in gratitude, the Rhode Islander moved to a Georgia rice plantation, where, in 1786 at the age of 43, he died reportedly of sunstroke.

Sir William Howe, accused of being one of the generals who lost the war, was found blameless after an investigation by Parliament. He later became an adviser (privy councilor) to King George III. He died at age 84.

Joseph Plumb Martin served through the war, reaching the rank of sergeant. He married and fathered five children. While town clerk of Prospect, Maine, he wrote poems, songs, and his memoir, considered one of the best sources of Continental Army life. He died in 1850 at age 89.

Albigence Waldo often suffered from illness while tending the sick at Valley Forge. He served in the Continental Army until October 1779, when he resigned because of ill health and returned to his native Connecticut, where he died in 1794 at the age of 44.

EDUCATIONAL EXTENSIONS

1. What is the "foreword" of a book? How does a book's foreword add meaning to the text? Read the foreword of *Remember Valley Forge* and research its author, Thomas Fleming. Why do you think he was chosen to write the foreword? What important background information did you gain about the topic?

2. How does the structure of the text contribute to the meaning and style? Describe the structure of *Remember Valley Forge,* including its use of illustration, photography, sidebars, and text. Give examples of how the presentation of information enhanced your understanding of the content.

3. How does an individual's personal experience enhance our understanding of history? Choose three personal accounts from the text and compare different perspectives on the war and happenings of the time. Distinguish between fact, opinion, and reasoned judgment. Analyze the relationship between primary and secondary sources.

4. Discuss Allen's characterization of George Washington, and cite primary and secondary sources that support or refute his claims.

More to ponder ...

- Why do authors write nonfiction? How can reading nonfiction shape our ideas, values, beliefs, and behaviors?

- What can we learn from reading real-life accounts of history? How are you affected when reading different points of view? How do the histories of earlier groups and individuals influence later generations?

- How has the world changed from the time period of the text? How do you think it will change in the future?

- Research a topic from the book. Compare and contrast information and details that you found from different sources.